人怎样能活到 150 岁

裴文瑾　朱婉斌　裴文璐　裴元照　裴元佑

How can human live up to 150 years old

Wenjin Pei　Wanbin Zhu　Wenlu Pei　Yuanzhao Pei　Yuanyou Pei

ISBN-13: 978-1541297043

ISBN-10: 1541297040

目录　Table of Contents

人怎样能活到 150 岁

1、前言

　　人的寿命本是与每一个人都有关系的问题，应该说很重要，每个人每天的生活与寿命都不能说没有联系，但是寿命有多长，一般人心目中是不考虑的，认为距今日生活太远，又寿命多长这个问题，人们早有固定看法，认为用不着操心，不要说一般人有此看法，即使是腰缠千百亿的老板，也是这样把寿命看穿了。但我们经过若干年的研究，反复思考，确信经过努力，会走到寿命大幅延长这一步，对国家、对社会乃至对人类尤其是对子孙后代是很重要的，故将我们的研究，以通俗的方式提供给人们，既给一般的人及有兴趣的人，也给那些在群体或国家中具有较多责任的人参考。我们之所以这样做，是因为我们是人类中的一分子，我们的目标是人类的长寿，和地球上绝大多数人的根本利益是一致的，后面所讲的问题，人类的后代子孙可能更受惠一些，这是长寿这件事的特点决定了的，实际上与今天人的长寿问题也是有关系的。

　　我们是根据物质世界中的物质变化科学地研究问题的，既不是什么帮派，也不是什么宗教，现今社会关于物质与精神有许多观点与解释，他们也有许多很好的愿望，对一些问题的认识与我们的认识不相同，我们的态度是，不论你执什么观点，只要对人类的生存与发展有利，都支持。

2、宏观地看一看人

本书理论的出发点是根据人们长久以来的经验及认识：在物质世界里"没有无物质的运动，也没有不运动的物质"。但这只是一个粗略的依据，为讨论下面的实际问题，引入了下面的现象：

"任何一个确定范围内的物质，总有某种邻近的物质存在，该确定范围内总有间断或连续地有物质流出到相邻物质，相邻物质也间断或连续地有物质流入到该确定的物质范围内"。

这个现象是很普通的，稍加注意就会感觉到它的存在，但没有更基本的定理来证明它，考虑到它究竟是一个很普通的现象，又下面的讨论要用到它，故称它为"平凡原理"，其中所说的间断或连续也包括多次的行为，例如吃饭、睡觉其动作是间断的同时也是多次的。下面我们就用上面的观点来宏观地看一看人。

首先，人是会动的东西，属于动物，当然任何物质都是在运动的，只是因为人及其他动物的动作相对所处的环境动得太明显而且有一定的自主性，故赋予一个专门的名称——动物。动物与其他物质的运动比起来，有一些现象动物显得很突出，几乎变成动物独有的，如动物都会进食及排泄，其他物质也有一定的吸收与排泄，但动物特别明显，为什么动物有此现象？根本原因在于动物会动，可以经常改变自己所处在的地方，身体可以随时改变位置，表面上看似乎与周围物质可以不相邻及不作物质交换，但按"平凡原理"，不作物质变换的物质是没有的，故动物连续或间断地进食与排泄这种明显的物质输入与输出动作，就是连续或间断地进行物质变换，这也是与外界物质联系的方式，与"平凡原理"是一致的，是动物在漫长的时间逐渐形成的动作。也是因为动物会动及觅食等生活需要，随时需要应付不同的环境，这比那些看起来几乎不动的物质需要应付的状况多而复杂，这种物质运动现象的累积，造成我们现在人称之谓头脑的东西或称智慧，但人的智慧比其他动物高出许多，为什么这种智慧最高的动物是我们这种两腿走路的动物——人类？而且是一枝独秀，不失一般性，我们可以设想人与其他动物在地球上生活之初的聪明与笨拙的程度差别并不大，但因人是用两脚走路，可以用手参与为生活而变换物质，使人所遇到的事物的复杂性是其他动物所没有的，使人的智力相对地提高得较快，由于智慧与智慧的发展是相辅相成的，即越有智慧则智慧也发展得越快，又因为人的智慧能继承，即后来人可以继承前人的智慧，在前人智慧的基础上获得更多的智慧，而其他动物在这点上与人相比差得很远，这些情况经过漫长时间的积累，造成人的智慧与其他动物的差别越来越大直到今天的程度。

人的智慧不仅表现在个人的力量上，还表现在能把许多个人的力量汇合成大许多倍的群体的力量，这也是人与其他动物的重要区别。人会逐步结成大小不同的群体，以至形成像现在的国家这样的大群体，由于群体与群体以及个人的利益，需要及思维不同，于是出现了群体与群体以及个人的矛盾及对立，今天地球上人类作为最聪明的所谓高级动物，实际上也是分成了许多对立的国家或集团，即使在一个国家内也是有不少利益不同而对立的群体，如果从人是如何从动物进化为人类分析，可以认为与人类的合作因素相比，许多对立属于人身上尚保留的动物因素之故，从人的总体利益看，它削弱了人类战胜自然的力量。

　　此外，人的聪明才智也大量用于相互斗争的手段上，尤其是像国家这样的大群体支持甚至本身就是侵略者的战争总是使地球上的人类丧失许多人的生命，后面我们会逐步讨论到如何对待及解决这一问题的看法。

3、人生中的生老病死及长寿事中有待改变的一些认识

人们通常说人生中少不了生、老、病、死四件大事，其中一般生都是好事，故大多数情况人们都能接受，除非同时带来了不幸的事为例外，老虽然意味着走向衰亡，但因是渐变，故在人的思想上一般反应不大，病虽不是好事，但也有一定的渐变，而且常常有希望改变，故在人的思想上虽有反应但常常不算很强，死通常是丧失，又常常是突变而不是渐变，这往往是使人们最为痛苦而难以接受的，因此要解决人生最为痛苦而难以接受的问题就是要解决死即长寿问题，先来看看目前在长寿问题上有待改变的一些认识，首先是认为100岁已经到头了，除了极个别人少许多一点，这是人类历史的经验，不能超过。还有些人认为传播了下一代后死亡是必然的，对死亡当然的认可，毫无异议地接受，认为只能举手投降，这个观念与上面的观念都认为不必为长寿及为永生奋斗。

另有一些人听说搞长寿时间很长，尤其听说自己又用不上，所以认为长寿不用搞，如果有现成的药丸则愿意采用，总之不想费事，也不想帮助别人，认为搞好自己现在的生活就行了，认为地球上的东西还不够用，寿命长了，人更多了，生活不好解决。

还有一些人认为只要爱国家就到头了，用不着爱人类，不知道爱国家与爱人类在通常的情况下是统一的。

还有的人，人数也不少，脑子里不是长寿问题而是明天的生活如何过下去的问题，包括打一天工吃一天饭的人，对这种人不能在思想认识上要求过高，而是应该由群体或社会关注他们。

还有一些人在社会上也不少，在社会上常常是随大流，生活过得也不错，算不上很好，自己也有少许力量帮助一下他人，但力量不大，有时出于人道，正义帮助一下他人，对长寿也可能有点兴趣。

还有一些人对人的生命的大幅延长更何况对永生是完全不信的，甚至对人类的永生也是没有信心的，这种人当然不会在追求长寿方面有所行动，认为没有必要去努力，我们认为这种思想是不战而降，但是我们对这些思想仍表示理解，首先我们不能要求他人和我们的看法一样，何况我们也没有能拿出实实在在的成绩去说服人家，只能要求我们自己把生命的大幅延长及永生这件事采取科学的态度作好作踏实及把我们的看法说出来供人们参考。

下面来谈一下有些人担心的寿命长了，人多了可能带来的生活问题，譬如说当在后面说的长寿社会开始了一段时期，由于人的合作关系的发展随之带来了智力提高，教育水平的提高，社会生产水平提高，寿命延长等的发展变化，人的寿命已有一些提高但还不是很高，譬如只提高了约十到二十岁，尚算不上大幅，可能有的人想到：地球上的物质，衣食住行能解决吗？又多了许多的人口往何处放？按我们的看法，这些仅仅是按现在人的生活环境及水平考虑的，如果考虑到人的智慧的发展，首先是上学的时间占人生的时间缩短了，但人的生活经验及智力积累大为扩充，人的生活方式由渐变积累起来而发生了许多变化，原来没住人的不少地方可住人了，整个人类的生活，远不是现在的生活水平，到时候都会有办法，人类生活的办法是随时都在调整的。

以上的思想认识都有可以继续改进尤其当长寿工作有一定进展时。但还有一些看似与长寿也有关系却不是一个简单的思想问题，譬如下面两种思想：

一是迷恋于核武器，妄图以此大规模消灭他人，及认为只有这样才能保护与发展自己，这与人类之中要减少对立是完全相反的；

另一种思想是认为现在世界上有一条没有写出明文的道理即：有理没理，以我是否打得过你为准，绝对化就变成强盗逻辑，为侵略者利用，完全是动物思维。

克服上面两种思想有一定难度，但是按照这里的看法，促其转变还是有可能的，长寿工作有助作到这一点。由于长寿工作是与每一个人都有关系的问题，会受到广大人民的支持，它的人民性决定了它的每一步的发展都会受到人们的关注，对每一个国家的人们都是很敏感的，如果某个国家或某个地方在此方面有所进步或走到了前头，对全世界的人都有一定的吸引力，这方面的信息和舆论对上面两种思想会产生无形的压力，因人心所向、人才、资金的流向使该国家更兴旺发达，人们都会很自然的希望这样的国家出来对世界多发挥作用。

长寿是人们天然的愿望，与整个人类的利益一致，在技术上也有一定的初步基础，由后面的叙述可以看到必须有一个和平的社会环境才会发展提高，在今天的人类世界，国家之间尤其是对世界有较大影响的国家及群体能坐下来商量消除对立，建立与发展世界和平，使人类能享受到长寿的幸福，确信这是人类的未来。

4、人类中尚存的动物特点妨碍了人类的发展进步

首先要解释一下两种不同的特点——人的特点与动物特点：

人是从动物的演变而来，人与其他动物在某些身体结构与器官上有某些相似是物质运动规律的结果，人在演变成今天的人的过程中，自身原来的动物特点逐渐减少，是因为人具有至今宇宙中其他物质所没有的能力，即学习及积累知识并传给下一代，弥补了知识不能直接通过肉体传给下一代的不足，以及人在能改变物质的能力中，包括与他人合作以使他人及自己改变物质的能力更大，并且愿意帮助他人甚至有时候当自己的利益和群体的利

益有某些不同会照顾群体利益。人的特点是指人的思维意识的特点而不是指皮肉构造，至于除人之外的其他动物，大家都见过，鸡、狗、松鼠等动物发现一块食物时常会叼到一角去吃以免它的同伴或其他动物来分享，成群的非洲的斑马如果遇到老虎来扑倒他们的同伴之一时不会回头来救被虎扑倒的同伴而是自己仍不停地继续往前跑，其实成百的斑马未尝不能对付得了一个老虎，这是因为动物没有这种认知，更不会将自己的认知传给下一代，一千年以前的老虎和现在的老虎的认知水平基本一样而现在的人比一千年以前的人的认知水平要高很多，对此这里将只顾自身不顾他人（或群体）利益称之谓动物特点。人是从动物演变过来的，自身的动物特点逐渐减少而成为现在人，也是经过学习及积累才具有人的特点的。

下面来看一个实际问题

人类社会可能已经发展了五千年以上，或者从有相当文化算起，大约也有三千年左右，经过这样长的时间还看不到寿命长到哪儿去，为什么现在能认为人类今后能作到寿命很长？回答是三千年的时间确实不短，人类在生产斗争及各方面的技能包括医治疾病方面都有一定进步，但看看人类的历史，在漫长的三千年中，人类将自己的精力用在对付自然方面的有多少，用在对付人的力量有多少，可以看到，虽然人是高级动物，应该是最懂在人与人的合作中 1+1 大于 2 的道理的，但事实上却是充满了许多巨大的群体之间的对立，精力大都放在如何将人类中的一部分人除掉（包括杀掉），历史成了少部分人的斗争史，几千年来人类内部的斗争大都并非广大人民群众之间有无法解决的仇恨需要拼你死我活，即这些斗争缺少人民性，根本不顾如何去改进与发展人与自然的斗争，与广大人们利益直接有关的长寿问题且不说千百年来改变不大，反而养成了什么一百岁到头了，死亡是必然的等许多思想障碍，又这些斗争大多数都是为了一少部分人的利益，所以这里说是人类在进化过程中尚存的动物特点妨碍了人类的发展，包括长寿事业的发展进步。

本来作为高级动物的人类是最懂同类之间合作的重要性的，但是如果看看其他动物的情况，同类也有互相伤害，低等生物也有相吃的，老虎虽吃一些其他动物，但老虎是少有捕杀老虎的，又斗争的规模及伤害同类的程度远不如人，人类中的斗争虽不是相吃，但许多时候也是要了对方的命。

如果这些因素也要计入到动物是否高级的比较的话，则人类的高级动物的桂冠恐怕要让给其他动物了。

5、人怎样能活到 150 岁

本书研究与讨论的人寿问题，寿命长短取多大范围是没有限制的，根据人认识物质世界中各种事物的规律，对于人寿这个具有无限长时间范围的问题作一定的分阶段，再通过积累而逐渐认识更大范围的事物也是人类认识事物的通常规律。至于为什么这里取 150 岁这个数字是因为人类至今活到 150 岁的人尚未出现过，到达此数字是一个有一定难度的进步，但较人类出现过的最高年龄也只有二十几岁，考虑到今天人类的发展状况，到达 150 岁这个数字也不是绝无可能，以吸取经验为日后作更大范围的研究，后面在讨论长寿工作的施行时也是取此数，可以认为如何活到 150 岁是目前有意义的现实问题。

　　人的寿命的延长，不同于通常的疾病采取一定的药物或手术可见功效，也不是像一些人想像的采取优越的衣食住行条件，甚至认为多积蓄些钱可"有钱能买鬼推磨"，实际上钱多不等于可以买到长寿。否则中国古代的皇帝，具有当时最优越的生活条件，结果寿命和普通人没有特别明显的差别，今天世界上前若干名的所谓首富，未听说比常人寿命长了多少，这里承认钱对人们有一定的帮助，但不是决定性的，寿命是涉及到自然与社会多方面知识的科学问题，不是某些特殊权力或经济地位就能做到的。做到长寿，既有个人的努力，也有推动群体的行为，人本是一种群体动物，多方面需要互相依靠的，人类是靠互相帮助做到所谓 1+1＞2 才获得发展的。按照这里的思想，物质变换是生命延续的基础，寿命延长要在物质变换上下功夫，在延长生命这方面的物质变换的水平上，目前在医学上已有相当高的水平，已可以变换除头部以外的身体各部分，还有消息变换头部也取得了很大进步，只是这些超乎通常水平的变换技术，尚未用到广大的每一个人身上，要改变这一点，就得群体乃至国家来想办法，采取配备一定的人员等措施，使广大的人们都能享受到目前已达到的物质变换的各种药物及手术的治疗。另外，个人也要有一定的努力，如果你真有心对长寿事业有一定兴趣，无论你原来是做什么工作，都可以花些功夫来做一些思考及研究，为果你能有这样的思维就更好了：即使将来用不到你自己身上而只能用到人的后代，当然也包括你的后代你也心甘情愿。

虽然每一个人都是群体中的人，许多事不能脱离群体这个大局，但是个人是不是就不能有所作为呢？回答是"否"。个人可以做的事很多，而且常常是群体行动必要的基础，但都离不开勤劳二字，有一句话应该是一个普遍适用的规律，与勤劳二字是一致的，即"动，才能继续动，不动就渐渐不能动了"，人体的各部分均是如此，脑力劳动及体力劳动都必须进行，脑力劳动看起来身体似乎未动，实际上思考问题时脑细胞也在运转，有一些劳动可能是有回报的，有些劳动表面上看按人们通常的观点对你似乎没什么好处，但有益于社会，也应该热心去做，在一个热心于公益的社会里，人人（包括你在内）都受益了，何况你的劳动也是有益于你的身体健康，这也是你得到的好处，据知社会上有不少这样的例子，一些人未老之前医院已查出其有若干老年病，后来因确信勤劳有助身体健康，每天坚持脑力劳动及体力劳动，坚持每天步行不少于2～4公里，最宝贵之处在于持之以恒，坚持一、二十年，不仅肚子上的多脂肪不见了，精神始终旺盛，思想上关注研究问题，越干越有劲，饭量也始终很好，身体默默地向超过百岁迈进，看样子比通常同龄人小约二十岁。

上面说的劳动不仅有益健康，对社会也有好处。另外，老人也应结合自己的情况总结点经验，有条件时也可写点文章，这既是劳动也是帮助他人，社会上需要劳动的事十分多，老人最好做到每天都闲不住，实际上对自己及对社会都好，生活内容也更加丰富。

包括老人在内我们今天享受的人类社会的文明，我们的知识、教育、物质生产与生活，以及身体某部分的器官坏了能够治疗，大都是我们的前人经过人与人的互助合作才创造出来并使我们得以享受的，我们现在生活着的人，在关注我们自己生活的同时，发扬人类发展必须具有的合作的特点，既是我们今天人的需要，也是使整个人类的文明得以继续保留。

今天的老人，在年青的时候，也是受到前人的关爱与培养，学到了许多知识，现在我们老了，社会尊重老年人是应该的，但老年人也要爱护年青人，爱护这个社会，将我们各方面的经验，传授给人们，使一代比一代强，这也是人间的合作关系，老人也有做不完的事情，也有学不完的新东西。

6、人类未来的长寿社会及长寿工作施行中的两步

6.1　什么是长寿

人们通常认为人的寿命不过百岁或稍多，如果在全世界寻找，大概可以找到个别的老人有 120 至 130 岁，找不到 150 岁的老人，但是按照这里所指的长寿，150 岁仅是下面第一步的目标，在这里，我们是科学地讨论问题，首先来谈一下死亡是怎么回事，因长寿与死亡是直接有关的。

由"平凡原理"知物质世界的任何一部分随时都在变化着，即任一时刻与此刻之前及之后都有一定改变，人们所称某一个名称的东西，都是指在某段时间内其变化在我们所研究与运用它的过程中，其改变的程度不影响该名称的使用。按此观点来看所谓死亡，就是指当变化到某一程度与过去相比差别很大以致不能容忍，才冠上"死亡"之词。这就是说人们定义的任何物质名称都只适用于该物质的一定变化区间。死亡及带来的困难是突变引起的。事实上，医学上的治病手段包括更换器官等也是经过改变物质变化来达到治病。长寿的第一步目标就是使人由出生到这一突变的时间尽可能长。

6．2 人类在整个物质世界中的优势

人类是宇宙中唯一的不是听天由命的物质，人类有一个任何物质都没有的优势，那就是能逐渐发现及利用物质运动的规律来为人类自己服务，以及人能通过教育将知识传给他人及下一代继续发展及提高。正如数学中的发散级数的级数和，比任何说出来的数字都要大，没有限制，因此，人的知识是累计的，其他任何物质包括其他动物都做不到这一点。

发散级数的性质，以发散级数

1，　1/2，　1/3，　　1/4，…，1/n，……

为例，级数的第 n 项为 1/n，初看此级数是逐项减小的，而且当 n 稍大，1/n 已很小了，但实际上当 n 相当大时，由 1 至 n 项的级数和会变得很大。

如果人的知识的级数是 a1，　a2，　a3，　a4，……，an，……

由 1 至 n 项的级数和是 a1+a2+a3+a4+……+an

如果此级数的每一项代表每一段时间（例如一年）科学知识取得的进步，容易想象到此级数后面与前面项的差别较前面级数的不仅减少得慢甚至是增加的，而且可能量还不小，即级数更是

发散的，人的知识累计得没尽头，科学知识丰富得难以想象。至于与人的寿命有何联系？由于用于医疗方面的知识常常是与整个科学知识，尤其是与人的生活及身体有关的科学同步或前沿，当医疗水平包括用于人体的物质变换的水平有所提高后，将使人的寿命也有一定的延长。

通常，能代表科学水平的级数和在一定的时间（例如一年）内都会有所增加，除人类或国家有重大事件的例外情况使科学技术的发展或方向有所改变，又上面的级数中的每一项也可看成是知识进步的记录，级数看成是文字记录的系列，级数和看成是记录的综合。

这里将人、群体均达到充分合作使科学技术发展到最高又人的寿命得以延长的社会称长寿社会。

上面说的是科学的道理，下面联系实际再予说明，按此情况，如果人在知识方面包括科学的进步，每一年都有所增加，人类社会已经发展了几千年，级数的发散特点早就应该显现出来了，人类的发达已经到难以估量的程度，为什么人类的寿命几乎停留在不过百岁？原因是这样，几千年的时间，人类的生产及科学相当大部分不是用在科学上，更不是用在与长寿有关的技能上，而是用在了属于上面所说的"例外情况"上，用在了人与人之间的斗争上，即用在了人类内部的对立上。医疗方面也不是像上面所说的科学技术的前沿，远没达到进入长寿社会必须的人、群体的充分合作，以使科学技术发展到最高使人的寿命得到相应的延长。

进入长寿社会，群体之间的表现是团结互助而不是互相压低，更不是你死我活的斗争，是人与人之间互相关心，乐于助人，尽最大的力量服务于社会，并发挥自己最大的创造力，使发散级数的每一项取得最大值，以使级数和取得最大值，即科学知识的发展及治病的水平也达到最高，因而人寿也得到最大的延长。

6.3　长寿工作的施行有两步

不论是否有条件进行如下的第一步都应采取身体各部多做运动的办法以助长寿，头脑的运动主要是思考问题，如果人体除头脑之外均能作物质变换，从技术上讲可以进入下面的第一步。

第一步的内容是：

1、人体物质变换的范围是除人脑以外的其他部分。

2、寿命延长到的范围大约是 120 岁以上，最高 150 岁。

这第一步寿命延长的程度不致使人口的矛盾太突出，且为空间技术的发展争取到一些时间，又老人们需要多锻炼自己的头脑以助将头脑能使用到 150 岁。

第一步另一件重要事情就是在科学技术上为下一步做准备，其中最主要的就是人脑的物质变换问题。

事实上，如果上面第一步的两项工作能完成，人类的寿命已有相当延长。

第二步的内容是：

人体的各部物质均可变换，在空间技术上已有很大发展的前提下，人类的生活空间已有很大扩展，人的寿命已向没有限制前进了不少，地球人已向作为宇宙人走了一步。

7、长远看人类能否避免死亡

这是针对近年来有不少书籍报刊谈的世界末日，认为人类灭亡的可能性很大，还列出了若干灭亡的方式等。这里并不认为这些说法全不正确，但认为所说的都是事件的危险性，很严重等，这里认为这只是问题的一面，这里抱科学态度讨论了问题的另一面，即人类能避免灭亡及人类永存的可能性，并认为通过人类的努力做到避免灭亡及人类永存是可能的。

7.1 如何理解"有生存就有灭亡"及"人类永存"的含义

这两句很普通的话看似有矛盾，因为前者说任何东西都有"死亡"而第二句话说"永存"这件事是存在的，这里认为物质世界的任何一部分随时都在变化着，即任何时刻与此刻之前及之后都有一定改变，人们所称的某一个东西的名称，都是人为定义的，故"有生存就有灭亡"这句话，就是指变化到某一程度，与过去相比差别很大就不能容忍，就冠上"灭亡"之词，这才引出了方便应用的"有生存就有灭亡"的说法，此说法作为描述物质一定时间区间的状态是可以的，作科学细致研究并不准确。

上面第二句话中的所谓永存，是指当物质恒保持均匀的变化而没有突变，宇宙中完全没有变化（变化有时也称运动）的物质是不存在的，即没有不运动的物质。

7.2 人类能避免灭亡的可能性是很大的

首先，正如前面在"人类在整个物质世界中的优势"中所说的人类知识水平及利用物质运动规律的不断提高，这为人类的永存创造了条件。

再者，根据目前谈到人类灭亡问题的报章书籍，能使人类灭亡的事件都不是立刻到来，往往最短也是一二百年以上甚至是数万年或更长的时间以后，即使只有一二百年对人类做准备来说也是相当长的，下面做一点粗略的估计。

在避免人类灭亡这件事上，人类的能力很大程度上决定于科技水平及物质生产水平，这是可想而知的，但是要预见一二百年内科技会有多少重大突破有一定困难，考虑到科技水平与物质生产水平本身也有相辅相成的关系，这里暂以物质生产水平做代表（当然这只是指人类能作寿命延长的潜力，是否用于长寿则是另一问题），譬如说，如果人类每一年的物质生产水平若提高2%，100年则可提高7倍，又如果每一年的提高为4%，则100年可提高50倍，可以看到，2%与4%都不是什么较高的数字，但由于2%与4%差了一倍，后果是50倍与7倍之差，这种差别很大程度上决定于人类自己，试想物质生产水平比今天高50倍的人类生活现在很难想象，但因今天已可做到少数人飞离地球一段时间，100年后人数肯定会增加许多，在空中呆的时间也很长，即使不能使大量的人搬家到其他星球上，也不会造成人类全部被毁灭。

由于我们是研究人类不被灭亡的可能性，根据目前所知的情况，时间区间 100 年尚属条件很好，如时间更长，倍数的差别会更大，由此可以看出在对付人类灭亡这件事上，人类自己的潜力是巨大的，但决定于人类是否齐心，否则可能大幅减少人类的力量，甚至使人类的力量不但不增加反而互相抵消。

7.3　避免人类灭亡的工作有可能带动人类或国家的较大发展

可能有人担心将力量用在比较遥远的避免人类灭亡的事件上会不会拉眼前工作的后退，这个问题可以分析一下，因为近期利益与长远利益也常有一致之处，有时长远目标会更加促进今天的工作，譬如地震，做好抵抗地震的工作是人类今日抵抗自然灾害的一个重要方面，如果要抵抗像当年恐龙遇到的由宇宙空间飞来的巨大陨石造成的地球上的超级大地震（造成了恐龙的灭亡），既是为解决今日在地球上遇到的地震问题，也有助人类发展飞向宇宙的空间技术，试想，当前通常一个地区地震过去之后，经过一些修复或再建之后还是要住人的，即仍在地球上，而现在的人类是否被灭绝的问题涉及到是否继续住在地球上或是大受限制了，必要时要大搬家到其他星球上或有相当长时间不在地球表面，这不是在讲天方夜谭而是地球上曾经发生过的严重事情，即恐龙灭亡的事，只是地球没有被全毁，经过漫长的时间又变成今天的面貌，解决这种问题，为了不使人类遭受灭顶之灾，人类就可能需要永久或暂时离开地球表面，这就需要发展太空技术，因不是只移动几个人而是众多的人，工作难度大很多，而发展太空技术既是今天的需要也是为避免人类灭亡的需要，涉及的科学门类十分多，将促进整个社会的全面发展，人们的物质生活水平也获得巨大的提高，可能有人会问，如果人类灭亡的事不发生，工作不是白费劲了吗？回答是这种工作往往会涉及到人类还没有的新知识新问题，有时还要动用不少物力财力，但远期及近期的利益都要照顾到，具体做的时候通常都要从小规模的实验开始，然后像"摸着石头过河"，按需要及力量考虑进一步的规模，至于人们为此事多费了劲，多费了脑筋，那就作为为子孙后代的幸福做了一些"前人栽树，后人乘凉"的事，大概也不会认为是"白做"。

这是以地震为例做的讨论，实际上地震只是许多需要做的工作的一个方面，人类可能被毁灭的方式也不限于这一个，还有核战争等更是在很大程度上是人类自己掌握的。

7.4 人类永存与人类中的个体即个人永存的若干关系

人类永存与人类中的个体的永存是不同的，人类永存是指这个大群体永久存在下去而不论其中的个体是一代一代地绵延下去的存在或是永久的并非一代一代往下传的方式存在。而个体永存是指人类中的个体（即个人）永久活下去而不出现"死亡"。人的生活本是群体的生活，人与人是互相帮助及互相依靠的，如果没有人类这个大群体的存在，也就谈不上个人的永存，故人类永存是个体永存的前提，从物质变化的角度来讲，个体存在与人类永存要求保持的状态是不同的，人类永存只需求人类整体有人继续而不管其中的个体是否存在"死亡"。人类永存与个体永存按前面长寿工作施行中的两步所述属长寿工作第二步的问题，但认识它们对整个长寿工作都是有必要的。

为配合前面关于人类未来长寿社会的叙述，下面按照人们普遍认知的人随年龄的增长面孔形象的变化绘了十六个由 120 岁到 150 岁的老人的面孔形象，前 8 个为女性，所表现的应该只是长寿社会初期的老人，因为正如寿命的延长一样，人的外观形象特别是老人会随科学特别是医学的进步而有一定的改变，会比这里画的美观。

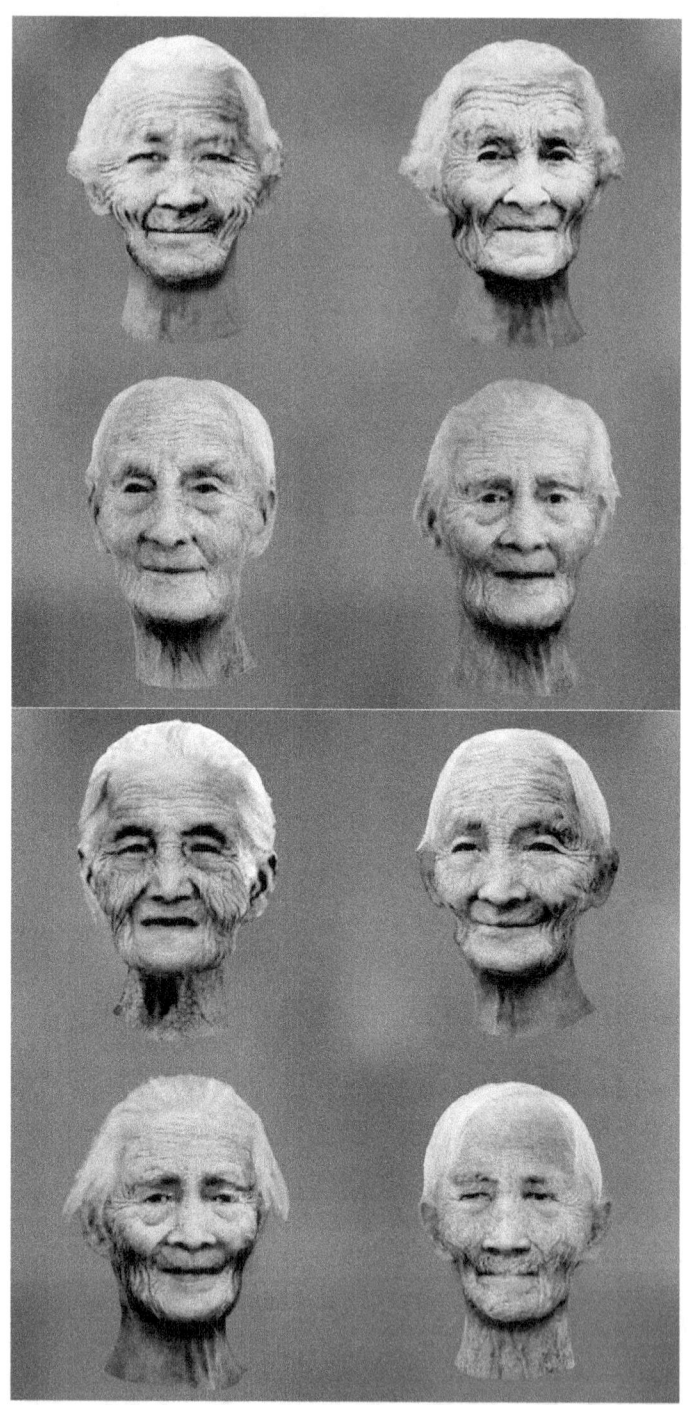

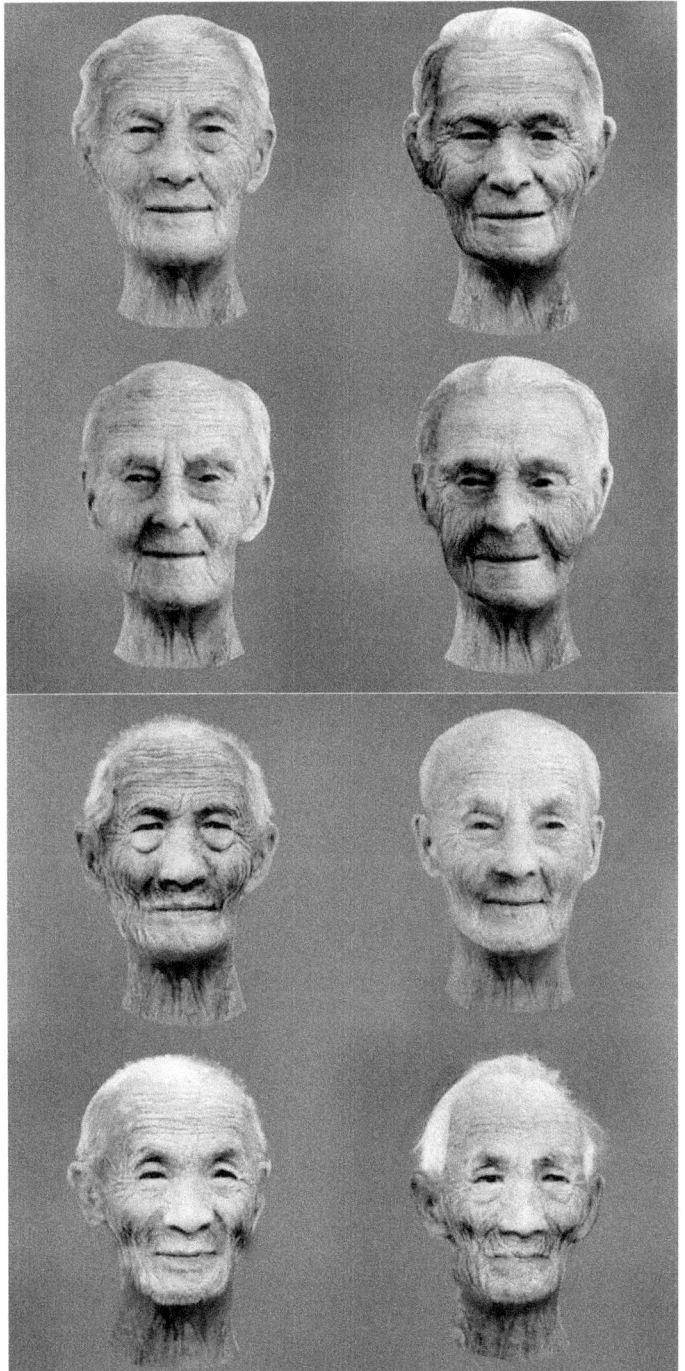

How can human live up to 150 years old

1. Introduction

Human lifespan is an important topic related to each individual. Everyday life of each individual affects his or her lifespan. However, most people do not pay attention to how long the lifespan actually is because they think it is far away from today's life. How long the lifespan is also considered by some people as a pre-determined subject and it is useless to for average people to think about it. Even millionaires and billionaires may think they have seen through the meaning of lifespan. But with years of studies, we are convinced that lifespan can be significantly extended if enough efforts are made. Lifespan is an important issue to societies, nationals, and especially important the coming generations. We present our studies in a plain language so that general public whoever interested and persons with important responsibilities in our government can use it as references. Our goal is to achieve longevity. This goal of achieving longevity is the same as the long lifespan goal of the majority of the human being. The topic discussed below will benefit the coming generations more because of the characteristics of the longevity; it also benefit the existing generations from longevity standpoint.

We study the development process of the physical world scientifically. We are not a branch of any cliques or religion groups. They have their own physical and spiritual opinions and explanations to the world we are living in. We may disagree their theories and thoughts. However we are not trying to prove their wrong as long as their views benefit the existing and developing of human being.

2. A macro view to human

The foundation of the theory described in this book is based on along-standing experience and awareness in the physical world: "No motion without matter; no matter without motion." But this is only a general statement. For the discussion of the following practical issue, let's consider this phenomenon:

"For any matter within a defined scope, there always exists of adjacent matters. Particles of the matter inside the defined scope transmit into the adjacent matters continuously or intermittently. And vice versa; particles of the adjacent matters transmit into the matter inside the defined scope continuously or intermittently"。

This is a very common phenomenon. You will notice its presence from your surrounding environments with a little attention. However there is no more fundamental theorem to prove it anymore because itself is a very basic phenomenon. This phenomenon will be used in the following discussion; and we give it a name, the "Ordinary Principles". The said "continuously" and "intermittently" includes multiple actions. For example, eating and sleeping are intermittent action, and at the same time they are multiple actions. Let's use the above theories to discuss the human being from a macro view.

First of all, please consider human as a moveable matter and one species of the animal world. All matter shave motions. And human and animals are moving and obviously related to surrounding environment. They move with certain autonomy and are classified as animals. Animal's motions are very prominent comparing to other matters if you consider eating and excretion as motions. These motions are unique for animals. Other matters have certain level of absorption and excretion too, but the animals' are particularly evident. Why animals have these phenomena? The fundamental reason is that animals are consistently changing their location and related positions. On the surface, it seems that they may not be adjacent to and exchange with surrounding materials. However, according to the "Ordinary Principles", no matter is without transmissions. The animal's continuous and intermittent feeding and excretion are obvious input and output action; they are continuous and intermittent material transmissions. This is the way animals connect to the outside world and is consistent with the "Ordinary Principle." It has gradually formed for a long time. Human will move and look for food. At any given time they will need to cope with different surrounding environment. These surviving conditions are much more complicated to deal with comparing to fixed matters' those do not need to deal anything. The accumulation of these complex movement phenomena of animal results in thing called brain or wisdom. Human's wisdom is much higher than that of other animals. Why human as animal has the highest wisdom? The two legs walking animal - human? And only the human. Without loss of generality, we can assume that human and other animals on the planet had a similar intelligent or clumsy level at the beginning. But human walk with two legs and leave hands to participate matter exchange for living. Thus, human can encounter things with much more complexities. Other animals do not. Thus human intelligence level has improved relatively faster. The improvement of people's intelligence is comparatively faster because the development of wisdom and intelligence are complementary; the more wisdom and intelligent, the faster the development of the wisdom and intelligent. Besides, human wisdom and intelligent can be inherited, later generations can obtain more wisdom and intelligent on the basis of previous generation's wisdom and intelligent. At this point, other animals are far worse when compared with human. After a long time accumulation, results in today's wisdom and intelligent level differences between human and other animals.

Human wisdom is not only in the power of each individual, but also in the capability of the combining the power of individuals into the group strength, which is also an important difference between human and other animals. Human gradually form groups of different sizes, from small communities to as large as nations.

Because interests, including ideologies, culture background and everyday needs, are different among the groups, opposition and contradiction emerge. Today, on the Earth, the human being, as the most intelligent animal, is actually divided into a number of rival countries or groups. Even inside a nation, there are a lot different interests opposition groups. If we analyze it from the point of view of how people have evolved from other animals, comparing to the character of collaboration, the oppositional character can be considered as the remaining that has inherited from animals. From the view point of overall human interest, it weakens the human power over nature.

In addition, human wisdom and intelligent are extensively used in fights or wars, especially the fights or wars supported by large groups or nations. The nations themselves are the invader causes that mankind lost much life on the Earth. Later, we will give our opinions on how to deal with and solve these problems.

3. Existing knowledge regards to human life and its life-span may need to change

General speaking, a life ultimately has four major events, birth, aging, illness and death. Wherein, the birth is generally considered as a good event unless, in rare events, it is a cause of a misfortune. The aging means progressing to dismal. But the aging process is a gradual process and causes no strong reaction in people's mind. The illness is not a good event. But it still has certain gradual and the expectation is that the illness condition may change, such as getting cured. The illness event may have some reaction in people's mind; but it is not considered strong event. The death is usually a lost. Most of the time, they are not gradual events. They are, unfortunately, sudden events which often make the most painful and difficult events to accept. To solve these most painful and difficult events is to solve the problem of death, or to become longevity. Let's take a look at current longevity mindset which needs to be changed.

First of all, 100 years old is considered as a limit, except for the rare cases. This is the experience of the human history. It cannot be exceeded. Some people think death is inevitable after the spread of the next generation. There is no objection to the recognition of the death. The only thing we can do is surrender. This concept refuses to put effort on longevity and eternity. Still others have heard that the study of longevity takes long time and may not useful for themselves and therefore the longevity studies do not need to be engaged. If there is an existing pills for the longevity, they are willing to adopt. In short, theydo not want any trouble;and do not want to help others. It is good enough if they can take care of themselves. They think there are not enough resources on the Earth. If the life span is longer, too many people will live on the earth and life may be getting difficult.

Some people think that it is good enough to love their country. No need to love mankind. What they do not know is that loving to country and loving to mankind under normal circumstances are unified.

There are also some people, actually a lot of them, have no longevity in their mind. What they think all the time is how to live tomorrow. This includes people who live paycheck to paycheck. For this group of people, they cannot be asked too much from their level of knowledge and should be cared by public and society.

There are also many people in our community who follow main streams. They live in a not-bad but not really good life. They may have some ability to help others, but not too much. Sometimes they may help others from humanity thought. They may have some interest on longevity.

There are some people who are totally unbelieving on the significantly extended human life, not even mention eternal life. They have no confidence on human eternal. Of cause, these people will not act on pursuing of longevity and think no need to work hard on this issue. This idea is giving up before the fight. We understand this thought. First, we cannot require others to have the same thought as ours and we do not have tangible results to convince them. What we can do is to do our best on the substantial extension of the life and getting the eternal life with a scientific attitude. People later on may use our example as reference.

Let's talk about people's worry about living conditions because of extended life. For example, a while after the longevity society started, the development of the human cooperation has brought in the improvement of intellect, raising of the education level, advanced social productivity and extended human life expectancy. Human life has been some extended but not much, such as 10 to 20 years, not a really substantial. Some people may question that do we have enough basic necessities, such as food, clothes and live space, etc.? Where the additional people to live? According to our thought, these concerns are merely based on current living standards and environment. The development of human wisdom and shortened school time will make person's life experience and intelligence accumulation greatly expended. Human life style changes because of the gradual accumulation. Some places where no human currently live can become livable. By the time the human life span is greatly extended, there will be resolution. People live habits can always be adjusted.

The theory mentioned above still has room to be improved, especially when there is progress on the study of the longevity. But there are seemingly longevity related and not a simple ideological problem, such as the following:

One is obsession of nuclear weapons and attempt to eliminate others in a large-scale. They think this is the only way to protect and develop their own. This is the exact opposition of the reduction of mankind antagonism.

Another unnamed standard is stronger one win, as long as I can beat you up. This is real a gangster's logic to clear the way for the aggressor. It is an animal thought process.

It is difficult to overcome these two theories. But we think it is still possible to. The studies of longevity can help. The studies of longevity relate to everyone and will get support from majority of the people. Its popularity determines that every step

of the development will attract people's attention. People from every country are sensitive to this topic. If any country or any region has improvements or advanced achievements, they will attract attention of the whole world. This information and media will form invisible pressure to the theories described above. Because people, intelligence and the flow of capitals will make the country more prosperity. People will naturally want this country standout and play more roles to affect the World.

Longevity is the people's natural desire. It is consistent with the interests of mankind as a whole. Besides, it has the preliminary technology basis. From the following discussion we will see that it needs a peaceful environment to develop and improve. In today's world, countries, especially large counties and groups who have relatively more effect to the world, can sit down and discuss ways to eliminate conflicts, establish world peace and let people enjoy happy longevity. We are convinced this should be the future of human being.

4. Some animal characters, which still exist in the human, prevent the human from development

First, let's explain two different characteristics - the characteristics of human and characteristics of animals:

Human was evolved from animals. The organs and structures similarities between human and other animals are the result of substance motion process. During the process of human evolutionary, its own original animal characteristics have gradually reduced. This is because the human has the capability to study and accumulate knowledge and pass the knowledge to next generations. This makes up the impossible of passing knowledge directly to the next generations through physical or genetic inheritance. Inside the capability of changing the world, human can cooperate with other human and enhance the capability of changing the world. The willingness to help others, and sometimes put group's interest in front of theirs even sometimes there is conflicts between his or her interests and group's interests.

The human characteristics refer to consciousness and logical thinking, not physical body structure. Other animals other than human, such as chickens, dogs, squirrels, etc., often eat their found food in a corner to avoid sharing. Large group of the

African zebra will continue to run away when their companion is attacked by a tiger. In fact, why cannot hundreds of zebra deal with a tiger? It is because animals do not have the knowledge and cannot pass the knowledge on to the next generation. The knowledge tiger has now and a thousand years ago are essentially the same. But the knowledge human has now is much more complex than that of a thousand years ago. Here we call the characteristic of which simply disregarding others interests the animal characteristic. The evolution of the human has gradually reduced this animal characteristic to become today's human. It is accumulated through learning process to become human.

Let's look at a practical issue.

Human society may have developed more than five thousand years, or about three thousand years since the date of considerable cultures. It still cannot see where the longevity goes, but why now it can forecast the longer life span? The answer is that three thousand years is not a short time. The
Humankind has made a concrete progress in skills of production and struggle as well as in each aspect including capability of curing diseases. But let's take a look at human history in this long 3,000 years, how much effort have been used to deal with natural environments and how much have

been used to deal with other people. Although human is a high intelligent animal and should understand that in people's cooperation 1 + 1 is greater than 2. But in fact there are so many conflicts between large groups of people. Most effort focused on how to get rid of others (including to kill). History has become the fighting history amount a small group of people. The fighting history about these several thousands of years is not about the unsolvable hatreds which need to fight to death. These fights lack of willingness of people and disregard how to improve the skills against the nature. The life expectation, which is related to the interest of majority of people, has not changed that much in last thousands of years. Even worse, it has form a thought disorder that maximum age is 100 years and death is inevitable. The fights or the wars were for the interest of small number of people. Therefore animal characteristics remained in the human hinder human development during the revolutionary, including the progress of longevity.

As a high intelligent animal, human should understand the most of the importance of cooperation inside of the same species. If you look at the case of other animals, there fights among the same species, lower organisms eat each other. Although tiger eats other animals, but the tiger rarely hunts tiger. And the hunting or fighting scales are much smaller than that of human. Human fights, though not to eat, are for kills most of the time. If considering this factor into how to classify the level of intelligence, the crown of high intelligence should give to other animals.

5. How can human live up to 150 years old.

This book focuses on research and discussion of the issue of the humankind's longevity, and how about the length of longevity is actually not restricted. In accordance with the rules concerning the humankind's cognition of various things in the material world, some specific analysis has been made in respect of infinite time range of the humankind's longevity, and furthermore, cognition of bigger range of things through accumulation is also the common rule of the humankind's cognition of things. Why is 150 years introduced here to discuss because the humankind hasn't lived to 150 years up to the present yet. And it is specifically difficult for the humankind to live to the above-mentioned figure, which is only more than 20 years' difference from the highest age appearing in the humankind, so it is not absolutely impossible for the humankind to live to 150 years in consideration of the today's status of development of the humankind. For purposes of absorb experience in order to make a bigger range of study in the future so the aforesaid figure is also used to discuss how to implement the longevity. And it may be thought that how to live to 150 years is presently a realistic issue for the humankind.

The extension of the humankind's longevity is different from common diseases, which are given drug or surgical

treatment to get good curative effect, and also not like adoption of excellent conditions of clothes, food, housing and travelling in some person's imagination, even not like thinking about saving much more money to reach "Money makes mare go". In fact, to save much more money is not quite equal to purchase of longevity. Otherwise, emperors or empresses in China's ancient dynasties, even if who had the most excellent living conditions at that moment, couldn't live a long life, resulting in having no explicit difference from that of general people. We don't basically hear that many so-called top plutocrats in today's world can live a longer life than common people. And I hereby acknowledge that money can play a specific role in extension of longevity, but isn't decisive. Longevity is a scientific issue involved in natural and social knowledge but can't be completed only with some special power or economic status. To make longevity is dependent upon either individual efforts or act of community promotion. The humankind is originally a group animal and need mutual reliance in many aspects. The humankind gets progressive development under mutual aid to make one plus one bigger than two. In accordance with the idea just talked about, the transformation of substances is the base of continuation of life, and extension of longevity should focus on the transformation of substances. As far as the level of transformation of substances is concerned in respect of extension of life, the humankind has reached the quite high level in medical respect, having been capable of changing all parts of body except the head. What's more, it is said that a big progress has been also made in change of head. Just these change technologies surpassing common level haven't been applied to each person yet. To change this point, the community or country has some ideas to adopt some measures to deploy some personnel in order to make a large population be able to enjoy various drug and surgical treatments brought about by change of substances. In addition, an individual also makes certain efforts. If you have an interest in research of the humankind's longevity, you will spend some time in doing some thinking and research whatever you are engaged in before. It will be better if you embrace the idea like that. Even if it will not be used by yourself but for the humankind's generations, it is certainly also for your generations, and you will then feel comfortable for that.

Although each person is one of the community and many things can't flee away from the community, can't an individual make any difference? The answer is "No". There are many things an individual can do, which are even the base of action of community, but everything depends upon "diligence". There is a saying that it should be a common rule and correspond with "diligence", that is, "to move is

the base of continuing movement, not to move will retrogress to failure of movement". Various parts of the humankind's body are also like this. Brain laborers and manual laborers must move, and brain laborers seem not to move in point of their bodies, their brain cells also work when thinking about problems. Some labor will probably receive remuneration, but some labor superficially seems not to bring any benefit for you according to the people's common viewpoints but is probably beneficial for the society. Therefore, we should be also enthusiastic to do them. In the society keen on the public benefits, each individual (including you) shall be benefited, and what's more, your work and labor shall be also conducive to your health, and this is also benefit you obtain. It is known that there are quite a lot of such examples as exists in the society. Some people have been examined to suffer from many senile diseases in the hospital before getting aged, and later deeply believe that hardworking is indeed conducive to health so they insist on doing some brain labor and manual labor every day and walking not less than 2-4kilometers every day. The most precious place lies in the persistence, and if a person is able to persist in ten or twenty years, redundant fat in his or her belly will disappear automatically, he or she will be always vigorous, can absorb himself or herself into research and keep energetic to do jobs and all the time have a good appetite,

resulting in quietly advancing to live to more than 100 years and usually looking about 20 years younger than some persons of the same age.

Labor mentioned above is not only beneficial for health but also conducive to the society. In addition, senior people should also sum up some experience in accordance with their own circumstances, and shall also do some writing when conditions permit, which is a kind of labor and also of help to other persons. There are too many things to be done in the society. Senior people had better work every day, which is actually good for themselves and the society in order to make living become richer and more excellent.

Including elderlies, we enjoy the civilization, intelligent, education, production and living qualify, and getting medical treatment when organs turn illness. Most of these benefits are from the creations of human cooperation. We, living people, need to promote the characteristic of that human development must have cooperation. It is what we need today, and it is to preserve and continue human civilization.

Today's elderlies got care and education from their predecessors, learned a lot. Now we are old. Society should respect the elderlies. The elderlies need to care young people,

care society, pass our knowledge to the next generation and make each generation stronger and stronger. This is the cooperation relationship among human. Elderlies have endless things to do and to learn.

6. The longevity societies in the future and two steps of implementing longevity

6.1 What is the longevity?

People normally believe that human life span is about hundred or slightly more. If looking around in the world, you may find several 120-130 years old individuals, but not a 150-year-old. What we think here in that life span of 150 years old is the first step. First let scientifically discuss what is death because death is directly associated to longevity.

From "Ordinary principles" we know that the whole physical world keeps changing. Any specific time is different from the moment before or after. When we name an object, it is the object which its changing does not affect the name even it is changing. Let's apply this to death. The change to the extent which cannot be tolerated, it is named "death". This is to say that naming is only valid when the object changes in certain scope. The death and difficulties from the death is a sudden event. In fact, medical treatment, include replacement organs, is achieved through changes in the material change. The first step is to make the process from birth to the "sudden event" as long as possible.

6.2 Advantages of mankind throughout the physical world

Human is the only object not resigned in the Universe. Human has an advantage no other objects have that human is able to gradually discover and utilize the laws of motion to serve the human being. And human will pass the knowledge to the later generations through education to develop and improve the knowledge. As in mathematics, the sum of the divergent series is larger than any numbers you can say and there is no limit. Human knowledge is cumulative. Any other objects, including other animals, cannot do this.

The character of the divergent series, let's use
1, 1/2, 1/3, 1/4, ..., 1 / n, ...

as an example, the n-th term is 1 / n. At first glance, this series is reduced one by one. When n is slightly larger, 1 / n is smaller. But when n is quite large, the sum of from 1 to n of the stage number becomes very large.
If the stage numbers of the human knowledge is a1, a2, a3, a4, ...,
an, ...
The sum of 1 to n is a1 + a2 + a3 + a4 + ... + an

If each stage number represents a period of time (eg. one year) of scientific knowledge acquired or advanced, it is easy to imagine the difference between this item and the item after this item reduces slower and even increase. And the amount may not be small because the series of the stage numbers are divergent. Human knowledge accumulation is endless and it is hard to imagine the amount of the knowledge can be accumulated. Regarding how this is related to the longevity? Because medical knowledge is often developing in parallel with all other technologies, especially technologies associated to human living and health. After the medical technologies, including matter transformation, have improved, human life span will have certain extension.

Typically, the stage numbers can represent scientific development and in a specific time (for example, one year) will increase. Major events in the human history or in the nation may alter scientific or technological developments. The above each number can also be seen as a record of advancement of knowledge. The numbers can be seen as a series of written records, and the series sum can be seen as a comprehensive record.

Here, the longevity society is defined as a society in which individuals and groups are fully cooperative and human life span have extended. What discussed above is scientific theory. Now let's talk about it from practical standpoint. Human society has been developed for thousands of years. The divergence of the series feature in terms of human society development shall have been emerged if the progress of knowledge, including science, increases annually, Human has developed into an inestimable level. Why life span still stays inside one hundred?

The reason is that significant production and science are not used in science field and not in longevity related skills, but used on the mentioned "exceptional circumstances" and used on the fight between people. It is used to against each other. Medical care is not at the cutting-edge as descripted. It is not get into the full cooperation required by longevity society So that science can developed to the highest level and extend human life span.

In longevity society, groups help each other rather than putting each other down. The relationship among individuals is caring and helpful. People use their best efforts to service the community and play to their maximum creativity so the divergent series get the maximum value. Scientific development and medical treatment technology reach the highest level, and thus life span get maximum extended.

6.3 Implementation of longevity studies has two phases

It doesn't matter if the condition exist or not to get into the first step should to keep exercise which help to extend the life span. Brain exercise is to think. If human body other than brain can all perform material transformation, technically you can get into the first step.

The first step is the content:

1.   The scope of material transformation is the body other than the human brain.
2.   The extension of the life span is approximately above120 years, up to 150 years.

This first step of the life extension does not result in a prominent contradiction in the expansion of population. It provides a timing space for technology development. Elderlies need to do more brain exercise to enable the brain to be used up to 150 years.

Another important thing in the first step is the preparation of science and technology for the next step. The most important matter is the material transfer issue of the human brain.In fact, if the two tasks in the first step are to complete, human life has been quite prolonged.

The content of the second step is:

Every part of the human body can be replaced. In the condition of the space development, the space for human live has been greatly expanded. Human life has advanced toward unlimited and the Earth human has one step further toward the Universe human.

7. In a long run, can human avoid death?

This is for the press in recent years. There are many books talking about apocalyptic, the possibility of human extinction and list of how. We do not think these claims are absolutely wrong. But the claims are only on one side. Let's take scientific approach to discuss this issue that human beings can avoid extinction through human efforts and eternal is possible.

7.1 How to understand "If there is living, there must be death." and "Human remains forever"

It seems like some contradictory between these two common sentences. The first sentence says everything has the end; and the second says human remains forever. We believe that the physical world is changing all the time. That is any time the moment before and after is different. The name of an object called by people is given by people. Therefore, the meaning of the death is called by people because the change to the certain extent that is so large and can be tolerated. That is the reason to conclude the usage of "If there is living, there must be death." It is possible to use this idea to describe a state of matter at certain time. However it is not accurate for detailed scientific studies.

The second sentence of the so-called forever refers to matters maintain a uniformly change without mutations. All matters in the Universe are changing and changing sometime is call movement. No matter that there is no movement.

7.2 There is very possible that human extinction can be avoided

First of all, as mentioned previously in the "human's advantage in the physical world", the continuous improvement of the human knowledge and skills in the use of the motion laws, it forms the conditions for human lasting forever.

Furthermore, according to the current discussions related to the human extinction in Medias and books, human extinction events are not coming at once. Often it has to be a minimum of one to two hundred years, or tens of thousands of years or even longer period of time. Even for only one or two hundred years, it is a long enough to from human to do the preparation. Below is a rough estimation.

In regards to the topic of avoiding human extinction, it is largely depended on technologies and productivity development. It is difficult to foresee major science and technology breakthrough for next couple of hundreds of years. Taking into account the technological development and productivities have a complementary relationship, let's use productivity as example (of course this refers to the potential of elongation of the human life. Whether it can be applied to longevity is another issue.). For instance, if the productivity increases by about 2% annually, it will increase by 7 times in 100 years; if the productivity increases by 4% annually, then it will increases by 50 times in 100 years. You can see, 2% and 4% are not significant numbers. Only because 4% doubles 2%, the consequences are 50 times versus 7 times. The difference is largely determined by human themselves. It is hard to imagine the human life in 50 time of today's productivities level. Today a few people may fly away from the Earth for a period time. In 100 years, the number of people may fly away from the Earth will certainly increase by a lot, and stay in the space for a longer time. Even they can move to other planet, it will not cause the destruction of mankind.

Since we are studying the possibilities of human not going extinction, 100 years time interval is good based on current known knowledge. If a longer time is employed, the difference of the multiples will be even greater. Thus the human being has enormous potential on dealing with the fighting against human extinction. However, it all depends on whether human can work together. Otherwise, it will greatly reduce human strength. The strength may not only be not increased, but also cancel each other.

7.3 The works to avoid human extinction may greatly drive the development of mankind and nationals

Some people may worry about that putting efforts on avoiding human distinction may interrupt the immediate works. We may analyze this concern. There are often consistencies between immediate and long-term interests. Sometimes, long-term goal will promote today's works. Let use earthquake as example. Preparation for the earthquake is an important aspect of human activities to fight natural disasters. Fighting the super earthquake dinosaur encountered then which caused by the huge meteorite from the space. Imagine the super earthquake which resulted in the demise of the dinosaur (Resulting in the demise of the dinosaurs) and solving the earthquake problem encountered on Earth today will help the development of the space technology used to bring people to the space. Imagine that after the earthquake, the same place will be re-built into livable space. It is still on the earth. However, the issue related to human extinction is the question about whether we can still stay on the earth; the option is limited. It may require us to move to other planet for a long time and not being able to stay on the earth. This is not talking about a fantasy but

a serious topic about an event actually happened on the earth, the demise of the dinosaurs. The earth was not been completely destroyed. After a long time, the earth becomes what it is today. In order to solve an event like this and avoid the human suffering the disaster, humans may need to permanently or temporarily leave the Earth's surface. This requires the development of space technology. Because it require moving a lot of people, not only a few, the task is much more difficult. The development of the space technology is not only a need for today; it is a need to avoid human extinction. This development involved a lot of scientific field, will promote the comprehensive development of the whole society, and improve people's living standards greatly. Someone may ask if will it be a waste if the demise of mankind never going to happen? The answer is that this research often involves new knowledge and new issues humans have not encountered. From practical standpoint It may need to start from a smaller scale experiment. And then, like searching the stones when crossing a river, consider further the size based on needs and resources. Like the story of the predecessors planted trees and descendants enjoy them, It is not a vain even if more effort and thought are spent for the happiness of the future generations.

The earthquake is used as an example for the discussion. However, the earthquake is actually only one of many aspect

works that need to be done. The way of human can be destroyed is not limited to this one. It may be others, such as nuclear war, which is largely controlled by human ourselves.

7.4 Relationship between mankind forever and individuals, and individual eternal.

The mankind forever is different from individual eternal. The mankind forever refers to the human race perpetuates forever as a species regardless the existence of individuals from generation to generation. The individual eternal means individuals live permanently without the occurrence of "death." Human life is the life of the community, people helping each other and relies on each other. Without the presence of this large human population, there are no individuals forever. Therefore the mankind forever is the premise of individual eternal. From material transformation perspective, the state of individual existence and the state of mankind forever is different. The human race perpetuates forever only requires the existence of the species regardless the individual death. The human race perpetuates forever and individual eternal are according to the second step of the two steps of implementing of longevity phases discussed previously. However, understanding of them is important for the studies of longevity issues.

As part of the description about the future longevity societies, the following are 16 portraits painted according to a general understanding of possible human face figure changes based on aging progresses from 120 to 150 years old. The first 8 figures are female.

They represent elderlies in the earlier stage of the longevity societies. As life expectancy increases, the appearances of the elderlies will change as the improvement of the technologies, especially in medical fields. They should be prettier than what presented here.

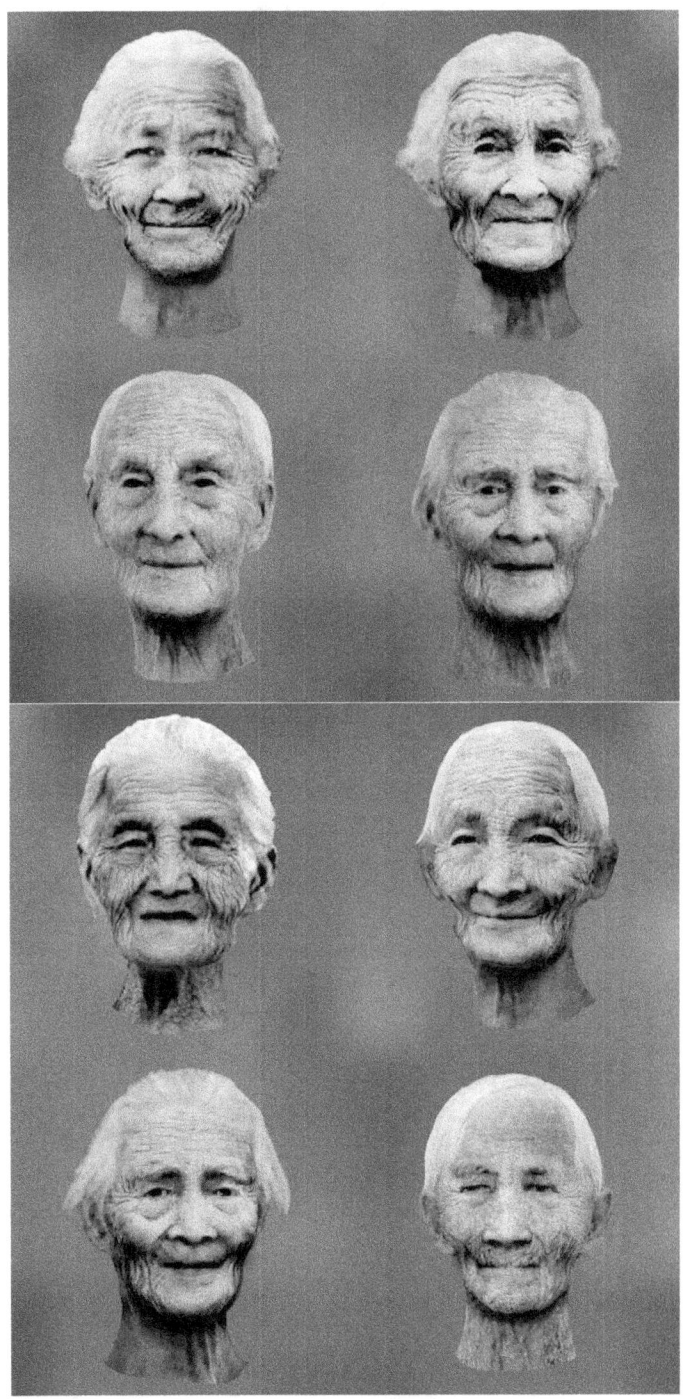

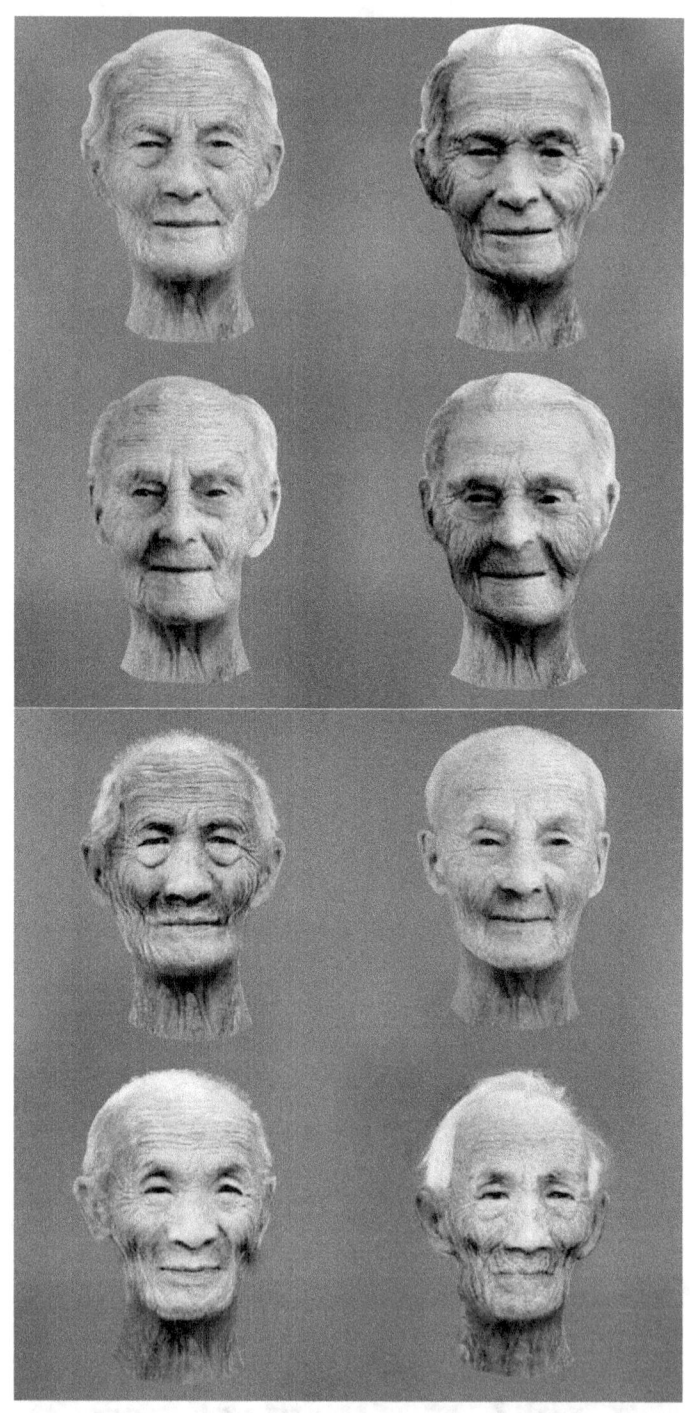

www.ingramcontent.com/pod-product-compliance
Lightning Source LLC
Chambersburg PA
CBHW060220290526
45789CB00003B/1341